MW01164692

To the man who pleases Him,
God gives wisdom, knowledge and happiness.

~ Eccles. 2:26 ~

_____

_____

_____

_____

_____

_____

_____

_____

_____

_____

_____

_____

_____

_____

_____

_____

_____

_____

_____

_____

Let us not become weary in doing good,
for at the proper time we will
reap a harvest if we do not give up.

~ Gal. 6:9 ~

Submit yourselves, then, to God.
Resist the devil, and he will flee from you.

~ James 4:7 ~

_____

_____

_____

_____

_____

_____

_____

_____

_____

_____

_____

_____

_____

_____

_____

_____

_____

_____

_____

_____

_____

_____

"Love one another. As I have loved you,
so you must love one another."

~ John 13:34 ~

If they obey and serve Him, they will spend the rest of
their days in prosperity and their years in contentment.

~ Job 36:11 ~

_____

_____

_____

_____

_____

_____

_____

_____

_____

_____

_____

_____

_____

_____

_____

_____

_____

_____

_____

_____

_____

_____

"All that the Father gives Me will come to Me,
and whoever comes to Me I will never drive away."
~ John 6:37 ~

_____

_____

_____

_____

_____

_____

_____

_____

_____

_____

_____

_____

_____

_____

_____

_____

_____

_____

_____

_____

_____

_____

But as for me, I watch in hope for the Lord,
I wait for God my Savior; my God will hear me.

~ Mic. 7:7 ~

_____

_____

_____

_____

_____

_____

_____

_____

_____

_____

_____

_____

_____

_____

_____

_____

_____

_____

_____

_____

_____

_____

Humble yourselves, therefore, under God's
mighty hand, that He may lift you up in due time.

~ 1 Pet. 5:6 ~

_____

_____

_____

_____

_____

_____

_____

_____

_____

_____

_____

_____

_____

_____

_____

_____

_____

_____

_____

_____

_____

The Lord will be your confidence and
will keep your foot from being snared.

~ Prov. 3:26 ~

_____

_____

_____

_____

_____

_____

_____

_____

_____

_____

_____

_____

_____

_____

_____

_____

_____

_____

_____

_____

_____

_____

Commit to the LORD whatever you do,
and your plans will succeed.

~ Prov. 16:3 ~

The Lord confides in those who fear Him;
He makes His covenant known to them.

~ Ps. 25:14 ~

_____

_____

_____

_____

_____

_____

_____

_____

_____

_____

_____

_____

_____

_____

_____

_____

_____

_____

_____

_____

_____

If the LORD delights in a man's way,
He makes his steps firm.
~ Ps. 37:23 ~

Trust in Him at all times, O people; pour out
your hearts to Him, for God is our refuge.

~ Ps. 62:8 ~

My flesh and my heart may fail, but God is
the strength of my heart and my portion forever.
~ Ps. 73:26 ~

Enter His gates with thanksgiving and His courts
with praise; give thanks to Him and praise His name.

~ Ps. 100:4 ~

_____

_____

_____

_____

_____

_____

_____

_____

_____

_____

_____

_____

_____

_____

_____

_____

_____

_____

_____

_____

Teach me to do Your will, for You are my God;
may Your good Spirit lead me on level ground.
~ Ps. 143:10 ~

———————————————————————

———————————————————————

———————————————————————

———————————————————————

———————————————————————

———————————————————————

———————————————————————

———————————————————————

———————————————————————

———————————————————————

———————————————————————

———————————————————————

———————————————————————

———————————————————————

———————————————————————

———————————————————————

———————————————————————

———————————————————————

———————————————————————

The Lord watches over all who love Him,
but all the wicked He will destroy.

~ Ps. 145:20 ~

_____

_____

_____

_____

_____

_____

_____

_____

_____

_____

_____

_____

_____

_____

_____

_____

_____

_____

_____

_____

"To him who overcomes, I will give the right to eat
from the tree of life, which is in the paradise of God."

~ Rev. 2:7 ~

_____

_____

_____

_____

_____

_____

_____

_____

_____

_____

_____

_____

_____

_____

_____

_____

_____

_____

_____

We know that in all things God works for the good
of those who love Him, who have been called
according to His purpose.

~ Rom. 8:28 ~

_____
_____
_____
_____
_____
_____
_____
_____
_____
_____
_____
_____
_____
_____
_____
_____
_____
_____
_____
_____
_____

May the God of hope fill you with all joy and peace
as you trust in Him, so that you may overflow with
hope by the power of the Holy Spirit.

~ Rom. 15:13 ~

_____

_____

_____

_____

_____

_____

_____

_____

_____

_____

_____

_____

_____

_____

_____

_____

_____

_____

_____

You have made known to me the path of life;
You will fill me with joy in Your presence.
~ Ps. 16:11 ~

I trust in Your unfailing love;
my heart rejoices in Your salvation.

~ Ps. 13:5 ~

Let the heavens rejoice, let the earth be glad;
let them say among the nations, "The LORD reigns!"

~ 1 Chron. 16:31 ~

Devote yourselves to prayer,
being watchful and thankful.

~ Col. 4:2 ~

_____

_____

_____

_____

_____

_____

_____

_____

_____

_____

_____

_____

_____

_____

_____

_____

_____

_____

To the man who pleases Him,
God gives wisdom, knowledge and happiness.

~ Eccles. 2:26 ~

_____

_____

_____

_____

_____

_____

_____

_____

_____

_____

_____

_____

_____

_____

_____

_____

_____

_____

_____

_____

Let us not become weary in doing good,
for at the proper time we will
reap a harvest if we do not give up.

~ Gal. 6:9 ~

_____

_____

_____

_____

_____

_____

_____

_____

_____

_____

_____

_____

_____

_____

_____

_____

_____

_____

_____

_____

_____

_____

Submit yourselves, then, to God.
Resist the devil, and he will flee from you.

~ James 4:7 ~

"Love one another. As I have loved you,
so you must love one another."

~ John 13:34 ~

If they obey and serve Him, they will spend the rest of
their days in prosperity and their years in contentment.

~ Job 36:11 ~

_____

_____

_____

_____

_____

_____

_____

_____

_____

_____

_____

_____

_____

_____

_____

_____

_____

_____

_____

_____

"All that the Father gives Me will come to Me,
and whoever comes to Me I will never drive away."
~ John 6:37 ~

_____

_____

_____

_____

_____

_____

_____

_____

_____

_____

_____

_____

_____

_____

_____

_____

_____

_____

_____

_____

But as for me, I watch in hope for the Lord,
I wait for God my Savior; my God will hear me.

~ Mic. 7:7 ~

Humble yourselves, therefore, under God's
mighty hand, that He may lift you up in due time.

~ 1 Pet. 5:6 ~

The Lord will be your confidence and
will keep your foot from being snared.

~ Prov. 3:26 ~

Commit to the LORD whatever you do,
and your plans will succeed.

~ Prov. 16:3 ~

The Lord confides in those who fear Him;
He makes His covenant known to them.

~ Ps. 25:14 ~

_____

_____

_____

_____

_____

_____

_____

_____

_____

_____

_____

_____

_____

_____

_____

_____

_____

_____

_____

_____

If the Lord delights in a man's way,
He makes his steps firm.

~ Ps. 37:23 ~

Trust in Him at all times, O people; pour out
your hearts to Him, for God is our refuge.
~ Ps. 62:8 ~

_____

_____

_____

_____

_____

_____

_____

_____

_____

_____

_____

_____

_____

_____

_____

_____

_____

_____

_____

_____

My flesh and my heart may fail, but God is
the strength of my heart and my portion forever.
~ Ps. 73:26 ~

Enter His gates with thanksgiving and His courts
with praise; give thanks to Him and praise His name.

~ Ps. 100:4 ~

_____

_____

_____

_____

_____

_____

_____

_____

_____

_____

_____

_____

_____

_____

_____

_____

_____

_____

_____

_____

_____

Teach me to do Your will, for You are my God;
may Your good Spirit lead me on level ground.

~ Ps. 143:10 ~

_____

_____

_____

_____

_____

_____

_____

_____

_____

_____

_____

_____

_____

_____

_____

_____

_____

_____

_____

_____

The LORD watches over all who love Him,
but all the wicked He will destroy.

~ Ps. 145:20 ~

_____

_____

_____

_____

_____

_____

_____

_____

_____

_____

_____

_____

_____

_____

_____

_____

_____

_____

_____

_____

_____

"To him who overcomes, I will give the right to eat
from the tree of life, which is in the paradise of God."

~ Rev. 2:7 ~

_____

_____

_____

_____

_____

_____

_____

_____

_____

_____

_____

_____

_____

_____

_____

_____

_____

_____

_____

_____

_____

_____

We know that in all things God works for the good
of those who love Him, who have been called
according to His purpose.

~ Rom. 8:28 ~

_____

_____

_____

_____

_____

_____

_____

_____

_____

_____

_____

_____

_____

_____

_____

_____

_____

_____

_____

May the God of hope fill you with all joy and peace
as you trust in Him, so that you may overflow with
hope by the power of the Holy Spirit.

~ Rom. 15:13 ~

_____

_____

_____

_____

_____

_____

_____

_____

_____

_____

_____

_____

_____

_____

_____

_____

_____

_____

_____

You have made known to me the path of life;
You will fill me with joy in Your presence.

~ Ps. 16:11 ~

_____

_____

_____

_____

_____

_____

_____

_____

_____

_____

_____

_____

_____

_____

_____

_____

_____

_____

_____

_____

_____

_____

I trust in Your unfailing love;
my heart rejoices in Your salvation.

~ Ps. 13:5 ~

Let the heavens rejoice, let the earth be glad;
let them say among the nations, "The Lord reigns!"

~ 1 Chron. 16:31 ~

Devote yourselves to prayer,
being watchful and thankful.

~ Col. 4:2 ~

To the man who pleases Him,
God gives wisdom, knowledge and happiness.
~ Eccles. 2:26 ~

_____

_____

_____

_____

_____

_____

_____

_____

_____

_____

_____

_____

_____

_____

_____

_____

_____

_____

_____

_____

Let us not become weary in doing good,
for at the proper time we will
reap a harvest if we do not give up.

~ Gal. 6:9 ~

Submit yourselves, then, to God.
Resist the devil, and he will flee from you.
~ James 4:7 ~

_____

_____

_____

_____

_____

_____

_____

_____

_____

_____

_____

_____

_____

_____

_____

_____

_____

_____

_____

_____

"Love one another. As I have loved you,
so you must love one another."

~ John 13:34 ~

_____

_____

_____

_____

_____

_____

_____

_____

_____

_____

_____

_____

_____

_____

_____

_____

_____

_____

_____

If they obey and serve Him, they will spend the rest of
their days in prosperity and their years in contentment.

~ Job 36:11 ~

_____

_____

_____

_____

_____

_____

_____

_____

_____

_____

_____

_____

_____

_____

_____

_____

_____

_____

_____

_____

"All that the Father gives Me will come to Me,
and whoever comes to Me I will never drive away."

~ John 6:37 ~

_____

_____

_____

_____

_____

_____

_____

_____

_____

_____

_____

_____

_____

_____

_____

_____

_____

_____

_____

_____

_____

But as for me, I watch in hope for the Lord,
I wait for God my Savior; my God will hear me.

~ Mic. 7:7 ~

Humble yourselves, therefore, under God's
mighty hand, that He may lift you up in due time.

~ 1 Pet. 5:6 ~

The Lord will be your confidence and
will keep your foot from being snared.

~ Prov. 3:26 ~

_____

_____

_____

_____

_____

_____

_____

_____

_____

_____

_____

_____

_____

_____

_____

_____

_____

_____

_____

Commit to the LORD whatever you do,
and your plans will succeed.

~ Prov. 16:3 ~

_____
_____
_____
_____
_____
_____
_____
_____
_____
_____
_____
_____
_____
_____
_____
_____
_____
_____
_____
_____
_____

The Lord confides in those who fear Him;
He makes His covenant known to them.

~ Ps. 25:14 ~

If the LORD delights in a man's way,
He makes his steps firm.
~ Ps. 37:23 ~

Trust in Him at all times, O people; pour out
your hearts to Him, for God is our refuge.

~ Ps. 62:8 ~

_____

_____

_____

_____

_____

_____

_____

_____

_____

_____

_____

_____

_____

_____

_____

_____

_____

_____

_____

My flesh and my heart may fail, but God is
the strength of my heart and my portion forever.

~ Ps. 73:26 ~

Enter His gates with thanksgiving and His courts
with praise; give thanks to Him and praise His name.

~ Ps. 100:4 ~

_____

_____

_____

_____

_____

_____

_____

_____

_____

_____

_____

_____

_____

_____

_____

_____

_____

_____

_____

_____

_____

Teach me to do Your will, for You are my God;
may Your good Spirit lead me on level ground.

~ Ps. 143:10 ~

The Lord watches over all who love Him,
but all the wicked He will destroy.
~ Ps. 145:20 ~

_____

_____

_____

_____

_____

_____

_____

_____

_____

_____

_____

_____

_____

_____

_____

_____

_____

_____

_____

_____

_____

_____

"To him who overcomes, I will give the right to eat
from the tree of life, which is in the paradise of God."

~ Rev. 2:7 ~

We know that in all things God works for the good
of those who love Him, who have been called
according to His purpose.
~ Rom. 8:28 ~

_____

_____

_____

_____

_____

_____

_____

_____

_____

_____

_____

_____

_____

_____

_____

_____

_____

_____

_____

_____

_____

May the God of hope fill you with all joy and peace
as you trust in Him, so that you may overflow with
hope by the power of the Holy Spirit.

~ Rom. 15:13 ~

You have made known to me the path of life;
You will fill me with joy in Your presence.

~ Ps. 16:11 ~

_____

_____

_____

_____

_____

_____

_____

_____

_____

_____

_____

_____

_____

_____

_____

_____

_____

_____

_____

_____

I trust in Your unfailing love;
my heart rejoices in Your salvation.

~ Ps. 13:5 ~

Let the heavens rejoice, let the earth be glad;
let them say among the nations, "The LORD reigns!"

~ 1 Chron. 16:31 ~

_____

_____

_____

_____

_____

_____

_____

_____

_____

_____

_____

_____

_____

_____

_____

_____

_____

_____

_____

_____

_____

_____

Devote yourselves to prayer,
being watchful and thankful.

~ Col. 4:2 ~

_____

_____

_____

_____

_____

_____

_____

_____

_____

_____

_____

_____

_____

_____

_____

_____

_____

_____

_____

_____

To the man who pleases Him,
God gives wisdom, knowledge and happiness.

~ Eccles. 2:26 ~

Let us not become weary in doing good,
for at the proper time we will
reap a harvest if we do not give up.

~ Gal. 6:9 ~

Submit yourselves, then, to God.
Resist the devil, and he will flee from you.

~ James 4:7 ~

_____

_____

_____

_____

_____

_____

_____

_____

_____

_____

_____

_____

_____

_____

_____

_____

_____

_____

_____

_____

_____

"Love one another. As I have loved you,
so you must love one another."

~ John 13:34 ~

If they obey and serve Him, they will spend the rest of
their days in prosperity and their years in contentment.

~ Job 36:11 ~

_____

_____

_____

_____

_____

_____

_____

_____

_____

_____

_____

_____

_____

_____

_____

_____

_____

_____

_____

_____

_____

"All that the Father gives Me will come to Me,
and whoever comes to Me I will never drive away."
~ John 6:37 ~

But as for me, I watch in hope for the LORD,
I wait for God my Savior; my God will hear me.

~ Mic. 7:7 ~

Humble yourselves, therefore, under God's
mighty hand, that He may lift you up in due time.

~ 1 Pet. 5:6 ~

The Lord will be your confidence and
will keep your foot from being snared.

~ Prov. 3:26 ~

_____

_____

_____

_____

_____

_____

_____

_____

_____

_____

_____

_____

_____

_____

_____

_____

_____

_____

_____

_____

_____

Commit to the LORD whatever you do,
and your plans will succeed.
~ Prov. 16:3 ~

_____

_____

_____

_____

_____

_____

_____

_____

_____

_____

_____

_____

_____

_____

_____

_____

_____

_____

_____

The Lord confides in those who fear Him;
He makes His covenant known to them.

~ Ps. 25:14 ~

_____

_____

_____

_____

_____

_____

_____

_____

_____

_____

_____

_____

_____

_____

_____

_____

_____

_____

_____

_____

_____

If the Lord delights in a man's way,
He makes his steps firm.

~ Ps. 37:23 ~

_____

_____

_____

_____

_____

_____

_____

_____

_____

_____

_____

_____

_____

_____

_____

_____

_____

_____

_____

_____

Trust in Him at all times, O people; pour out
your hearts to Him, for God is our refuge.

~ Ps. 62:8 ~

My flesh and my heart may fail, but God is
the strength of my heart and my portion forever.

~ Ps. 73:26 ~

Enter His gates with thanksgiving and His courts
with praise; give thanks to Him and praise His name.

~ Ps. 100:4 ~

Teach me to do Your will, for You are my God;
may Your good Spirit lead me on level ground.

~ Ps. 143:10 ~

The Lord watches over all who love Him,
but all the wicked He will destroy.

~ Ps. 145:20 ~

_____

_____

_____

_____

_____

_____

_____

_____

_____

_____

_____

_____

_____

_____

_____

_____

_____

_____

_____

_____

_____

_____

"To him who overcomes, I will give the right to eat
from the tree of life, which is in the paradise of God."

~ Rev. 2:7 ~

We know that in all things God works for the good
of those who love Him, who have been called
according to His purpose.

~ Rom. 8:28 ~

May the God of hope fill you with all joy and peace
as you trust in Him, so that you may overflow with
hope by the power of the Holy Spirit.

~ Rom. 15:13 ~

_____

_____

_____

_____

_____

_____

_____

_____

_____

_____

_____

_____

_____

_____

_____

_____

_____

_____

_____

_____

You have made known to me the path of life;
You will fill me with joy in Your presence.

~ Ps. 16:11 ~

I trust in Your unfailing love;
my heart rejoices in Your salvation.

~ Ps. 13:5 ~

_____

_____

_____

_____

_____

_____

_____

_____

_____

_____

_____

_____

_____

_____

_____

_____

_____

_____

_____

_____

_____

Let the heavens rejoice, let the earth be glad;
let them say among the nations, "The Lord reigns!"
~ 1 Chron. 16:31 ~

Devote yourselves to prayer,
being watchful and thankful.

~ Col. 4:2 ~

To the man who pleases Him,
God gives wisdom, knowledge and happiness.

~ Eccles. 2:26 ~

Let us not become weary in doing good,
for at the proper time we will
reap a harvest if we do not give up.

~ Gal. 6:9 ~

Submit yourselves, then, to God.
Resist the devil, and he will flee from you.
~ James 4:7 ~

_____

_____

_____

_____

_____

_____

_____

_____

_____

_____

_____

_____

_____

_____

_____

_____

_____

_____

_____

_____

_____

"Love one another. As I have loved you,
so you must love one another."

~ John 13:34 ~

If they obey and serve Him, they will spend the rest of
their days in prosperity and their years in contentment.

~ Job 36:11 ~

"All that the Father gives Me will come to Me,
and whoever comes to Me I will never drive away."
~ John 6:37 ~

But as for me, I watch in hope for the LORD,
I wait for God my Savior; my God will hear me.

~ Mic. 7:7 ~

Humble yourselves, therefore, under God's
mighty hand, that He may lift you up in due time.

~ 1 Pet. 5:6 ~

_____

_____

_____

_____

_____

_____

_____

_____

_____

_____

_____

_____

_____

_____

_____

_____

_____

_____

_____

_____

_____

_____

The LORD will be your confidence and
will keep your foot from being snared.

~ Prov. 3:26 ~

Commit to the LORD whatever you do,
and your plans will succeed.

~ Prov. 16:3 ~

The LORD confides in those who fear Him;
He makes His covenant known to them.

~ Ps. 25:14 ~

_____

_____

_____

_____

_____

_____

_____

_____

_____

_____

_____

_____

_____

_____

_____

_____

_____

_____

_____

_____

_____

If the Lord delights in a man's way,
He makes his steps firm.
~ Ps. 37:23 ~

_____

_____

_____

_____

_____

_____

_____

_____

_____

_____

_____

_____

_____

_____

_____

_____

_____

_____

_____

_____

Trust in Him at all times, O people; pour out
your hearts to Him, for God is our refuge.

~ Ps. 62:8 ~

My flesh and my heart may fail, but God is
the strength of my heart and my portion forever.

~ Ps. 73:26 ~

_____

_____

_____

_____

_____

_____

_____

_____

_____

_____

_____

_____

_____

_____

_____

_____

_____

_____

_____

_____

Enter His gates with thanksgiving and His courts
with praise; give thanks to Him and praise His name.

~ Ps. 100:4 ~

Teach me to do Your will, for You are my God;
may Your good Spirit lead me on level ground.

~ Ps. 143:10 ~

_____

_____

_____

_____

_____

_____

_____

_____

_____

_____

_____

_____

_____

_____

_____

_____

_____

_____

_____

_____

_____

The LORD watches over all who love Him,
but all the wicked He will destroy.

~ Ps. 145:20 ~

"To him who overcomes, I will give the right to eat
from the tree of life, which is in the paradise of God."

~ Rev. 2:7 ~

We know that in all things God works for the good
of those who love Him, who have been called
according to His purpose.

~ Rom. 8:28 ~

_____

_____

_____

_____

_____

_____

_____

_____

_____

_____

_____

_____

_____

_____

_____

_____

_____

_____

_____

_____

May the God of hope fill you with all joy and peace
as you trust in Him, so that you may overflow with
hope by the power of the Holy Spirit.

~ Rom. 15:13 ~

You have made known to me the path of life;
You will fill me with joy in Your presence.

~ Ps. 16:11 ~

I trust in Your unfailing love;
my heart rejoices in Your salvation.

~ Ps. 13:5 ~

_____

_____

_____

_____

_____

_____

_____

_____

_____

_____

_____

_____

_____

_____

_____

_____

_____

_____

_____

_____

_____

Let the heavens rejoice, let the earth be glad;
let them say among the nations, "The Lᴏʀᴅ reigns!"

~ 1 Chron. 16:31 ~

Devote yourselves to prayer,
being watchful and thankful.

~ Col. 4:2 ~

To the man who pleases Him,
God gives wisdom, knowledge and happiness.

~ Eccles. 2:26 ~

_____

_____

_____

_____

_____

_____

_____

_____

_____

_____

_____

_____

_____

_____

_____

_____

_____

_____

Let us not become weary in doing good,
for at the proper time we will
reap a harvest if we do not give up.

~ Gal. 6:9 ~

Submit yourselves, then, to God.
Resist the devil, and he will flee from you.

~ James 4:7 ~

_____

_____

_____

_____

_____

_____

_____

_____

_____

_____

_____

_____

_____

_____

_____

_____

_____

_____

_____

_____

_____

"Love one another. As I have loved you,
so you must love one another."

~ John 13:34 ~

If they obey and serve Him, they will spend the rest of
their days in prosperity and their years in contentment.

~ Job 36:11 ~

_____

_____

_____

_____

_____

_____

_____

_____

_____

_____

_____

_____

_____

_____

_____

_____

_____

_____

_____

_____

"All that the Father gives Me will come to Me,
and whoever comes to Me I will never drive away."

~ John 6:37 ~

But as for me, I watch in hope for the LORD,
I wait for God my Savior; my God will hear me.

~ Mic. 7:7 ~

Humble yourselves, therefore, under God's
mighty hand, that He may lift you up in due time.

~ 1 Pet. 5:6 ~

The Lord will be your confidence and
will keep your foot from being snared.

~ Prov. 3:26 ~

_____

_____

_____

_____

_____

_____

_____

_____

_____

_____

_____

_____

_____

_____

_____

_____

_____

_____

_____

_____

_____

Commit to the Lord whatever you do,
and your plans will succeed.

~ Prov. 16:3 ~

_____

_____

_____

_____

_____

_____

_____

_____

_____

_____

_____

_____

_____

_____

_____

_____

_____

_____

_____

_____

_____

The Lord confides in those who fear Him;
He makes His covenant known to them.

~ Ps. 25:14 ~

_____

_____

_____

_____

_____

_____

_____

_____

_____

_____

_____

_____

_____

_____

_____

_____

_____

_____

_____

If the LORD delights in a man's way,
He makes his steps firm.

~ Ps. 37:23 ~

Trust in Him at all times, O people; pour out
your hearts to Him, for God is our refuge.

~ Ps. 62:8 ~

_____

_____

_____

_____

_____

_____

_____

_____

_____

_____

_____

_____

_____

_____

_____

_____

_____

_____

_____

_____

_____

My flesh and my heart may fail, but God is
the strength of my heart and my portion forever.

~ Ps. 73:26 ~

Enter His gates with thanksgiving and His courts
with praise; give thanks to Him and praise His name.

~ Ps. 100:4 ~

Teach me to do Your will, for You are my God;
may Your good Spirit lead me on level ground.

~ Ps. 143:10 ~

_____

_____

_____

_____

_____

_____

_____

_____

_____

_____

_____

_____

_____

_____

_____

_____

_____

_____

_____

_____

_____

_____

The LORD watches over all who love Him,
but all the wicked He will destroy.
~ Ps. 145:20 ~

_____

_____

_____

_____

_____

_____

_____

_____

_____

_____

_____

_____

_____

_____

_____

_____

_____

_____

_____

_____

"To him who overcomes, I will give the right to eat
from the tree of life, which is in the paradise of God."

~ Rev. 2:7 ~

We know that in all things God works for the good
of those who love Him, who have been called
according to His purpose.

~ Rom. 8:28 ~

_____

_____

_____

_____

_____

_____

_____

_____

_____

_____

_____

_____

_____

_____

_____

_____

_____

_____

_____

_____

May the God of hope fill you with all joy and peace
as you trust in Him, so that you may overflow with
hope by the power of the Holy Spirit.

~ Rom. 15:13 ~

You have made known to me the path of life;
You will fill me with joy in Your presence.

~ Ps. 16:11 ~

I trust in Your unfailing love;
my heart rejoices in Your salvation.

~ Ps. 13:5 ~

_____

_____

_____

_____

_____

_____

_____

_____

_____

_____

_____

_____

_____

_____

_____

_____

_____

_____

_____

Let the heavens rejoice, let the earth be glad;
let them say among the nations, "The LORD reigns!"

~ 1 Chron. 16:31 ~

Devote yourselves to prayer,
being watchful and thankful.
~ Col. 4:2 ~

To the man who pleases Him,
God gives wisdom, knowledge and happiness.
~ Eccles. 2:26 ~

Let us not become weary in doing good,
for at the proper time we will
reap a harvest if we do not give up.

~ Gal. 6:9 ~

_____

_____

_____

_____

_____

_____

_____

_____

_____

_____

_____

_____

_____

_____

_____

_____

_____

_____

_____

_____

Submit yourselves, then, to God.
Resist the devil, and he will flee from you.

~ James 4:7 ~

_____

_____

_____

_____

_____

_____

_____

_____

_____

_____

_____

_____

_____

_____

_____

_____

_____

_____

_____

_____

_____

"Love one another. As I have loved you,
so you must love one another."

~ John 13:34 ~

If they obey and serve Him, they will spend the rest of
their days in prosperity and their years in contentment.

~ Job 36:11 ~

_____

_____

_____

_____

_____

_____

_____

_____

_____

_____

_____

_____

_____

_____

_____

_____

_____

_____

_____

_____

_____

"All that the Father gives Me will come to Me,
and whoever comes to Me I will never drive away."

~ John 6:37 ~

But as for me, I watch in hope for the LORD,
I wait for God my Savior; my God will hear me.

~ Mic. 7:7 ~

_____

_____

_____

_____

_____

_____

_____

_____

_____

_____

_____

_____

_____

_____

_____

_____

_____

_____

_____

_____

Humble yourselves, therefore, under God's
mighty hand, that He may lift you up in due time.

~ 1 Pet. 5:6 ~

The Lord will be your confidence and
will keep your foot from being snared.
~ Prov. 3:26 ~

_____

_____

_____

_____

_____

_____

_____

_____

_____

_____

_____

_____

_____

_____

_____

_____

_____

_____

_____

_____

Commit to the LORD whatever you do,
and your plans will succeed.

~ Prov. 16:3 ~

The LORD confides in those who fear Him;
He makes His covenant known to them.

~ Ps. 25:14 ~

If the Lord delights in a man's way,
He makes his steps firm.
~ Ps. 37:23 ~

Trust in Him at all times, O people; pour out
your hearts to Him, for God is our refuge.

~ Ps. 62:8 ~

My flesh and my heart may fail, but God is
the strength of my heart and my portion forever.

~ Ps. 73:26 ~

Enter His gates with thanksgiving and His courts
with praise; give thanks to Him and praise His name.

~ Ps. 100:4 ~

_____

_____

_____

_____

_____

_____

_____

_____

_____

_____

_____

_____

_____

_____

_____

_____

_____

_____

_____

_____

_____

_____

Teach me to do Your will, for You are my God;
may Your good Spirit lead me on level ground.
~ Ps. 143:10 ~

The LORD watches over all who love Him,
but all the wicked He will destroy.

~ Ps. 145:20 ~

_____

_____

_____

_____

_____

_____

_____

_____

_____

_____

_____

_____

_____

_____

_____

_____

_____

_____

_____

_____

"To him who overcomes, I will give the right to eat
from the tree of life, which is in the paradise of God."

~ Rev. 2:7 ~

_____

_____

_____

_____

_____

_____

_____

_____

_____

_____

_____

_____

_____

_____

_____

_____

_____

_____

_____

We know that in all things God works for the good
of those who love Him, who have been called
according to His purpose.

~ Rom. 8:28 ~

_____

_____

_____

_____

_____

_____

_____

_____

_____

_____

_____

_____

_____

_____

_____

_____

_____

_____

_____

_____

May the God of hope fill you with all joy and peace
as you trust in Him, so that you may overflow with
hope by the power of the Holy Spirit.

~ Rom. 15:13 ~

_____

_____

_____

_____

_____

_____

_____

_____

_____

_____

_____

_____

_____

_____

_____

_____

_____

_____

_____

_____

_____

You have made known to me the path of life;
You will fill me with joy in Your presence.

~ Ps. 16:11 ~

_____

_____

_____

_____

_____

_____

_____

_____

_____

_____

_____

_____

_____

_____

_____

_____

_____

_____

_____

_____

I trust in Your unfailing love;
my heart rejoices in Your salvation.

~ Ps. 13:5 ~

_____

_____

_____

_____

_____

_____

_____

_____

_____

_____

_____

_____

_____

_____

_____

_____

_____

_____

_____

_____

Let the heavens rejoice, let the earth be glad;
let them say among the nations, "The LORD reigns!"

~ 1 Chron. 16:31 ~

Devote yourselves to prayer,
being watchful and thankful.

~ Col. 4:2 ~

To the man who pleases Him,
God gives wisdom, knowledge and happiness.

~ Eccles. 2:26 ~

_____

_____

_____

_____

_____

_____

_____

_____

_____

_____

_____

_____

_____

_____

_____

_____

_____

_____

_____

Let us not become weary in doing good,
for at the proper time we will
reap a harvest if we do not give up.

~ Gal. 6:9 ~

Submit yourselves, then, to God.
Resist the devil, and he will flee from you.

~ James 4:7 ~

_____

_____

_____

_____

_____

_____

_____

_____

_____

_____

_____

_____

_____

_____

_____

_____

_____

_____

_____

_____

_____

"Love one another. As I have loved you,
so you must love one another."

~ John 13:34 ~

If they obey and serve Him, they will spend the rest of
their days in prosperity and their years in contentment.

~ Job 36:11 ~

_____

_____

_____

_____

_____

_____

_____

_____

_____

_____

_____

_____

_____

_____

_____

_____

_____

_____

_____

"All that the Father gives Me will come to Me,
and whoever comes to Me I will never drive away."

~ John 6:37 ~

But as for me, I watch in hope for the Lord,
I wait for God my Savior; my God will hear me.

~ Mic. 7:7 ~

Humble yourselves, therefore, under God's
mighty hand, that He may lift you up in due time.

~ 1 Pet. 5:6 ~

_____

_____

_____

_____

_____

_____

_____

_____

_____

_____

_____

_____

_____

_____

_____

_____

_____

_____

_____

_____

_____

The LORD will be your confidence and
will keep your foot from being snared.

~ Prov. 3:26 ~

Commit to the Lord whatever you do,
and your plans will succeed.

~ Prov. 16:3 ~

_____

_____

_____

_____

_____

_____

_____

_____

_____

_____

_____

_____

_____

_____

_____

_____

_____

_____

_____

The Lord confides in those who fear Him;
He makes His covenant known to them.

~ Ps. 25:14 ~

If the Lord delights in a man's way,
He makes his steps firm.
~ Ps. 37:23 ~

Trust in Him at all times, O people; pour out
your hearts to Him, for God is our refuge.

~ Ps. 62:8 ~

My flesh and my heart may fail, but God is
the strength of my heart and my portion forever.

~ Ps. 73:26 ~

Enter His gates with thanksgiving and His courts
with praise; give thanks to Him and praise His name.

~ Ps. 100:4 ~

Teach me to do Your will, for You are my God;
may Your good Spirit lead me on level ground.

~ Ps. 143:10 ~

_____

_____

_____

_____

_____

_____

_____

_____

_____

_____

_____

_____

_____

_____

_____

_____

_____

_____

_____

_____

The LORD watches over all who love Him,
but all the wicked He will destroy.

~ Ps. 145:20 ~

"To him who overcomes, I will give the right to eat
from the tree of life, which is in the paradise of God."

~ Rev. 2:7 ~

We know that in all things God works for the good
of those who love Him, who have been called
according to His purpose.

~ Rom. 8:28 ~

May the God of hope fill you with all joy and peace
as you trust in Him, so that you may overflow with
hope by the power of the Holy Spirit.

~ Rom. 15:13 ~

You have made known to me the path of life;
You will fill me with joy in Your presence.

~ Ps. 16:11 ~

_____

_____

_____

_____

_____

_____

_____

_____

_____

_____

_____

_____

_____

_____

_____

_____

_____

_____

_____

_____

_____

I trust in Your unfailing love;
my heart rejoices in Your salvation.

~ Ps. 13:5 ~